Crushing Debt

9 Strategies to Eliminate Financial Bullies

Table of Contents

Foreword

If you have ever experienced financially difficult times in your life due to a large reduction in income, frivolous spending in college, or racked up medical bills that were more than your budget could bear, you know the extreme emotional upset that occurs when bill collectors are calling you. After all, you are an honest person and really want to be debt free or at least in a positive cash flow with all your debt paid. But due to your particular circumstances, no matter how many calculators you use, the answer is the same: there is more cash going out than is coming in.

If you want to emotionally disconnect from the collection bullies who call you day and night, review the situation from a basis of logic, not emotion, and put a proven plan into place to get out of this debt nightmare, then this book is for you. As a Creditor Harassment Attorney, Shawn can help you determine your next steps to avoiding sleepless nights, sort out real debt from Zombie debt, and break down your debt problems into manageable steps forward.

Reading through Shawn's fabulous book I realized that no matter how much I know about debt and credit, I too have faced times when I needed an outside opinion, someone who was not emotionally attached to my problems. A mentor, a professional with a track record of reducing the emotional and financial stress and terror when your money no longer stretches and your debt skyrockets, that is who Shawn is. This book could not come at a more critical time to help people manage their debt problems.

I knew after reading the first few chapters that Shawn understands the emotions around debt: confusion, guilt, panic attacks, helplessness and embarrassment. He unwinds debt situations into bite-sized manageable steps to help you move toward a calm resolution.

Crushing Debt is a wonderful book. It's about real solutions to managing unpaid debts and past financial problems that haunt you today. It is full of personal stories, case studies and practical tips to provide insight into how lenders look at your debt with a very different lens.

As I age I have learned a very important lesson: you cannot solve the debt problem you have with the same thinking you used when you got into debt.

I urge you to read this book, and if the unresolved debt you are facing now is more than your nerves and stomach can bear, then contact Shawn@Yesnerlaw.com and let the master handle the collection bullies and get you back on the road to financial peace.

Wishing you financial peace,

Polly A. Bauer, CPCS
Past President CEO of The Home Shopping Network Credit Corporation
Author, Speaker, Consultant and Founder of Polly Bauer and Associates, Inc.
Creator of Swipe! The Podcast, a podcast to help people be credit savvy

Introduction

This is a book about bullying. Wait, the title is "Crushing Debt." How does that relate to bullying?

Growing up, I was tormented by bullies, actually one bully in particular. By the time I stopped growing I was 5 feet 8 inches tall, and significantly shorter than that in Junior High School and the beginning of High School. I was skinny, and a smart and sarcastic kid. I didn't get into any major trouble, I was always home on time to do my homework and study, and I rarely took risks (I'm risk-averse even today, starting my own business and writing this book notwithstanding). I was also in the band. Now, before you start on the "this one time, in band camp" stories, know that my bullies were also in band with me. Luckily my best friend, who I am still friends with today, was captain of the football team, the wrestling team and baseball team – so the jocks never picked on me, knowing they would have to answer to him.

However, my high school bully, who would also be with me as a member of the Florida State University Marching Chiefs, made sure I was kicked, punched, and covered in masking tape (at that time I had a full head of hair). I was intentionally almost run over by him while he was driving his car and I was walking to school one day (I lived less than two blocks from my high school). I had my personal stuff broken, stolen, thrown away and destroyed. I was peer-pressured and made fun of by people who I thought were my friends. Unfortunately, I never stood up for myself in any of those situations.

Why do I say all of this when this is not a book about psychology? Fast forward to today – my bully and I are friends! Well maybe not friends, but friendly. I see him from time to time while tailgating in Tallahassee for Florida State University college football games and occasionally, I'll go see his band play a gig when I'm in Tallahassee (which I visit quite often, as an alumnus, and because my sister, her family, and my parents all now live in Tallahassee).

Today, I tell my clients that one benefit of hiring me is that I can take the emotion out of their situation to give them clear legal advice. That's close to the truth because if you really want me to take on your case, if you really want me emotionally invested in your case, then tell me your story from a perspective of you being bullied. I'll be instantly transformed into that scared junior high / high school kid trying to get through the day without being bullied, although now twenty-plus years' more experienced and confident than my pre-teen and teenage self.

Do you have credit card companies chasing you for payment? Do you have "junk debt" buyers and their collection agencies calling you? Are you afraid of zombies (or zombie debt)? Has a collection company called (or sued) to collect a debt that does not belong to you? Are your wages being garnished? Do you get calls at all hours of the day and night? Does your family get calls from people trying to find you? Does your cell phone ring constantly from creditors trying to get ahold of you? Have you asked the creditors to stop calling without success? Do you have mounting hospital bills? Or credit card bills? Do you wonder how you're going to make your mortgage payment? Do you have to choose between paying the credit card bill and eating dinner? Do you hold your breath when paying by credit card because you're at, or over, your limit? Are you in foreclosure or is a foreclosure imminent? Is your student loan payment equal to or more than your car payment or your house payment? Does the IRS keep your tax refund, without making a dent in what you owe to the Federal Government? Do you want those "financial bullies" to go away?

If the answer to any of these questions is "YES" then this book is for you.

Finally, one question I ask most of my clients, "At the end of the month do you have money left over, or at the end of the money do you have month left over?"

During my career, I've helped my clients eliminate millions of dollars of debt by negotiating with their creditors, suing their creditors, filing bankruptcy for my clients, or sometimes a combination of those strategies. I wrote this book for people that have month left at the end of the money. I wrote this book for people who feel bullied by their creditors. I wrote this book for people who feel afraid, intimidated, and scared by their creditors. This book is my chance to help others eliminate their financial bullies. When you've finished this book, I hope you think to yourself "everything is going to be okay."

At the end of each chapter, we will provide some tip, tactic or strategy to help you eliminate the financial bully associated with that chapter. You could just skip to the end of each chapter, but my hope is that you'll read each chapter, then incorporate my **Crushing Debt Tip** into your financial strategy.

I'll tell stories where appropriate to illustrate a point. These stories are 100% true, except I have changed or left out my client's name, and sometimes the names or identities of other parties to adhere to the ethical standards of the Florida Bar. As a practicing attorney, I still have an ethical obligation to maintain attorney-client privilege. Speaking of, while the stories are true, they are not indicative of results I can get for any client. Each client, creditor and fact pattern are different and so "your mileage may vary." In that same vein, this book is not a substitute for legal advice, as your situation will differ from what I discuss in this book. If you have questions, please contact our office or contact a local attorney, especially if you reside outside the state of Florida.

One more thing before we get started, each of the chapters has some commonality, so rather than retype the same thing in every chapter, I'll provide these common themes here in the introduction:

1. Call the creditor and ask for help. Most bullies don't like confrontation and asking your creditors what you

can do to resolve the situation could create quick and easy solutions.

2. Contrary to popular opinion, it is a myth that everything on the Internet is true. Sarcasm here, but the "internet attorney" is rarely correct or accurate. As one of my networking partners says, "the only thing more expensive than hiring a professional is doing it yourself."

3. Call a professional in your area for help if you get stuck. Most people are afraid or embarrassed to ask for help. I have file cabinets full of files in my office and have no opinion (or no negative opinion) about my clients. Sometimes bad sh-tuff happens to good people. My goal is to help you, rather than look down on you after you've made a few poor choices or been impacted by forces outside of your control.

So, with those ground rules ...

Chapter 1 - Debt Settlement, It Ain't Poker

In poker, people sometimes bluff when they have a bad hand, hoping the other players can't read the truth and will surrender the chips they've already played although they have the better hand. In settling debt, bluffing rarely works because most of the time the borrower lacks leverage, and bluffing can seriously backfire on you. But there are multiple solutions available, which we'll talk about in depth in this book.

I've helped many clients settle their debts when bankruptcy was a bad option or when bankruptcy was simply an option the client discounted for another reason.

I've often said to clients that convincing a creditor to take less than what is owed is not poker. Sure, there may be some bluffing involved; a majority of the time, however, we believe that full disclosure is a more effective technique than withholding information. If we've got the winning hand, we tell the world, often and with conviction. Debt negotiation is not criminal law – there is no such thing as "innocent until proven guilty" or in debt settlement terms "unable to pay until proven an ability to pay." In fact, it is the opposite – debt collectors will try to repossess assets, garnish wages, or levy against bank accounts until the borrower proves those assets are exempt, over-encumbered by debt, or simply not worth pursuing. The debt collectors have "heard it all before" so they're unlikely to be swayed by any argument other than facts (and sometimes not even facts will dissuade them from attempting to collect). Therefore, disclosing the nature of your assets, although it reveals their existence to the creditor, also shows the creditor that those assets are protected, unavailable for forced collection, or simply not worth pursuing.

Recently, a client told me they would refuse to provide a spouse's information for fear that the lender would pursue the unemployed spouse for debt collection, on a debt that was incurred prior to the marriage. While we respect that decision, we think it was wrong for two reasons: (1) the spouse had no obligation, thus no liability to the creditor, so providing the spouse's information posed no danger to assets owned individually by the spouse. Providing her information to the creditor would have been as "dangerous" to her as providing my information to the creditor, that is, it would have had no impact. Neither me nor the spouse owed the creditor money. (2) Because the spouse was unemployed, providing her information to the creditor would have proved that the husband (the borrower) was exempt from garnishment as the Head of Household.[1]

If you end up going to court and losing, or if you ignore the lawsuit and a judgment is entered in favor of the creditor, the borrower is required to provide a Fact Information Sheet[2] and failure to do so will possibly create penalties of contempt or other sanctions

---

[1] Under Florida law, the Head of Household provides more than one-half of the support of dependents. §222.11, Florida Statutes

[2] Florida Rules of Civil Procedure Form 1.977

against the borrower by the judge (which in the most extreme or egregious cases would include jail). In many cases, providing the information will assist us in the settlement of the debt and, in rare cases, cause the creditor to drop collection activities entirely. We had one client who did have the creditor stop calling after we disclosed that the client: (1) was a realtor during the recent Great Recession, (2) who had no pending listings, (3) had no IRA, 401(k), savings, or money in the bank and (4) was unable to find employment. What the creditor didn't know was that this client lived with his significant other, who was taking care of all or most of his expenses. Accordingly, we haven't heard from the creditor, as of the time of drafting this chapter, in over five (5) years, and it's unlikely we'll ever hear from this creditor again!

If you want to be prepared, or are just curious and you want to see a copy of the Fact Information Sheet, please email me at Shawn@YesnerLaw.com and include "Fact Information Sheet" in the subject line. The

Fact Information Sheet requests information such as (this is an incomplete list, see the Fact Information Sheet for more details):

- Legal Name and Aliases
- Residence Address
- Employment Information, including rate of pay and commission structure
- Social Security number and Driver's License number
- Marital Status and spouse's employment information (if applicable)
- Information about children that live with you
- Real estate you own
- Motor vehicles you own

Certainly, there are creative ways to answer questions included on the Fact Information Sheet; although we would never endorse or recommend lying to the creditor on this form because it is requirement of the court and lying on this form could be criminal perjury (even a lie by omission – "they never asked for that information.") However, presenting the information in such a way that the creditor sees the borrower's assets are non-existent, or exempt, or that secured assets are upside down (more is owed than the value of the property) will go a long way towards a quick and easy settlement – and if that information is provided at the outset of our negotiations, that's even better.

Some other information you may want to consider providing to the creditor, to show that you are "uncollectible" include:

- Three (3) to six (6) months of bank statements,
- Two (2) years of previous tax returns,
- A profit and loss statement if you own your own business,
- Pay stubs if you are a W-2 employee,
- Proof of other debt or judgments you have against you (the maximum garnishment is 25% of income from any source, so if one creditor is garnishing the maximum 25% then no other creditors can garnish until the first is repaid),

- Proof of any alimony or child support you pay, and
- A hardship letter (more about the hardship letter in the loan modification chapter.)

What happens if you have assets and/or the creditor finds out about assets you own? Florida law (or the law of your home state) protects your property by exemption[3].

Currently, Florida law provides the following exemptions:

- Equity in your homestead (primary residence) is 100% exempt[4]
- Wages of the Head of Household[5]
- Life Insurance policies[6]
- Annuity contracts[7]
- Disability income[8]

---

[3] Chapter 222, Florida Statutes
[4] §§ 222.01 and 222.02
[5] §222.11
[6] §222.13
[7] §222.14
[8] §222.18

- IRA, 401(k) or other retirement account[9]
- Money in a qualified tuition program, medical savings account and similar programs[10]

This is not a comprehensive list and I would encourage you to talk to a local attorney to determine if you have exemptions to protect your property, especially if you live outside the state of Florida.

Many times, my advice to a client depends on whether the client has a "thick skin." If the client is un-phased by creditor collection calls, if the client has no fear of a lawsuit because they have nothing the creditor can take, then we can negotiate with the creditors to settle the debt. If, on the other hand, the client is tired of being bullied by creditors or simply wants to avoid the hassle of talking to the debt collectors, then bankruptcy may be a better option.

---

[9] §222.21
[10] §222.22

Along the same lines, for a debt settlement to be an effective strategy, the client must have money saved that they can use to settle with the creditors. Typically, we can settle with the debt collectors for our clients to pay anywhere between 25 and 35% of what they owe to pay off the debt so that the collectors leave them alone, unless we're dealing with a credit union (who typically never settle) or American Express (who rarely accepts less than 90% of what is owed).

Also, we are **_NOT_** a debt settlement company that takes monthly payments each month and accumulates money to then offer the creditors in settlement. These companies are frequently scams and the first few years' worth of payments are typically used to pay their fees. Instead, we are suggesting that you save your money and once we negotiate a settlement with the creditor that is affordable for you, at that point, you pay the money and settle the account.

Finally, most people are afraid, or bullied by the incessant calls they receive from a debt collector. In Chapter 3, we'll discuss the FDCPA (Fair Debt Collection Practices Act) and the FCCPA (Florida Consumer Collection Practices Act), but for purposes of this chapter, once you let the debt collector know that you are represented by an attorney, they are unable to call you directly and must communicate with you through your attorney. For communications after the attorney's notice of representation, the creditor might be liable to the borrower for damages of $1,000, or $500 - $1,500 per call made to a cell phone!

Crushing Debt Tip

In most cases, full disclosure is a more effective technique than withholding information. When the creditor knows you have nothing to give, that there is no pot of gold at the end of your rainbow, they will likely leave you alone, or set themselves up to be sued for over-aggressive debt collection practices (more on that in coming chapters).

Chapter 2 - Dealing with Zombie Debt

What is Zombie Debt? My non-legal definition is that Zombie Debt is debt that has been written off, discharged or eliminated, but because it was transferred from collection agency to collection agency (sometimes transferred four or five times or more!), borrowers still get calls trying to collect on that debt – debt that has risen from the grave!

Zombie Debt might be eliminated with various consumer protection laws like the FDCPA (Fair Debt Collection Practices Act), the FCCPA (Florida Consumer Collection Practices Act)[11], the TCPA (Telephone Consumer Protection Act) and all those cool acronyms that we attorneys like to throw around that basically are designed to prevent improper, illegal, or overly aggressive debt

---

[11] If you live outside of Florida, consult a local attorney to see if you have a similar state-specific consumer protection law.

collection activities (which we'll get into in the next chapter).

If I get a client that has settled, paid off or otherwise eliminated a debt, and they get a call from another collector, I instantly send out a letter to the creditor to verify the debt and to stop calling the client.

Even better, if I send out that letter, and I show the collection agency where the debt was satisfied, I can set up the creditor for more egregious violations for trying to collect a bad debt, which may entitle my client to a statutory $1,000 penalty and the creditor will pay me my attorney's fees. If the debt was eliminated or discharged in a bankruptcy, even better, because then I can go to the federal bankruptcy court, re-open the case and have the bankruptcy court sanction the creditor (more money for the client).

Recently, I dealt with two different types of zombie debts:

In the first case, a client received a letter from a collection agency, attempting to collect a student loan debt. The problem is that the client's father paid the student loan debt, in full, eight (8) years earlier! I sent the creditor a nice letter – I call them cease & desist or "C&D" letters, or sometimes I call them "nasty-grams." Luckily for my client, he saved every shred of evidence I needed to make a strong case that this debt was paid in full. As attachments to my letter, I sent the collection company the written pay off letter from eight years ago, and a copy of the check showing payment. I was also able to send the front and back copy of the check, to show the creditor that one of its predecessors had cashed the check. It's been a few years but, so far, no further contact from the creditor. Unfortunately, this is likely the best we can expect, as the creditors do not send "sorry, we were wrong" letters or any other type of confirmation, unless we sue them. In this case the client wanted to send the letter before considering whether to file a lawsuit.

If you email me at Shawn@YesnerLaw.com and put in the subject line "C&D Letter," I can send you a copy of my letter.

In the second case, my client modified his home mortgage. As part of the modification, the bank took a huge chunk of the arrears and put that balance due at the end of the loan. Years after the modification, the bank waived that "deferred balance" and issued my client a 1099-C Forgiveness of Debt form, causing my client to have to report forgiveness of debt income. At the time, the Mortgage Debt Relief Act existed and prevented my client from paying any taxes on that income. Years later, the client came to me to file bankruptcy, because he had again fallen behind in payments on his home mortgage. When we filed the Chapter 13 repayment plan, the creditor filed a claim *including* the amount previously waived (the "deferred balance"). In other words, the bank waived the deferred balance, issued a 1099c for the deferred balance, and then tried to double back and collect the deferred balance! I filed an objection to the claim and fought with the bank. The challenge I had was the conflicting case law between Pennsylvania, Tennessee, and the other states, and as of the publication of this book, no Florida appellate court nor the Florida Supreme Court has had this issue come before it for a decision.

In re: Zilka[12], is a Pennsylvania case that argues that the 1099c is merely a reporting device and not evidence that the debt is eliminated. This is the majority view amongst the states that have decided the issue. This is contrast with *In re: Reed*[13], a Tennessee case that argues that the 1099c does eliminate the obligation of the taxpayer / borrower to repay the debt.

Again, Florida has not decided the issue, and the U.S. Supreme Court has not reconciled the difference of opinion between the states, therefore I was faced with the options of: (1) forcing the bank to back down, (2) advising my clients to back down, or (3) making new case law in the state of Florida. Fortunately

---

[12] 407 B.R. 684 (W.D. Penn 2009)
[13] 492 B.R. 261 (E.D. Tenn 2013)

(or unfortunately, depending on your point of view) we played chicken with the bank and they gave in! The bank amended its bankruptcy claim to remove that portion of the debt that was "deferred balance" thus reducing the amount of money owed by my client! Although we didn't get the judge to issue a ruling that our interpretation of the law was correct we did get the desired result, that the amount written off via the 1099c was no longer collectible, so I'm counting that as a win and my client sure thought so!

Crushing Debt Tip

Keep track of all of your old debts that are written off, paid off, discharged in bankruptcy, too old, or eliminated in some other way. If they come back to life, if a creditor contacts you to collect that money, there are some great tools to erase this Zombie Debt!

Chapter 3 - Keep Your Call Log

As of March 2018, the United States Federal Reserve shows that there is over $3.8 trillion of consumer credit outstanding![14]

Although failing to pay your Visa® bill (regardless of how much) will have virtually no impact on whether Visa® survives as a company, I think we can all agree that there is a TON of debt out there, and debt collectors will do nearly anything to get it.

The Fair Debt Collections Practices Act (FDCPA)[15] was created by the United States Congress to combat the "abundant evidence of abuse, deception and unfair debt collection practices by many debt collectors."[16] Congress found that abusive debt collectors contribute to the number of individual bankruptcies, divorce, loss of jobs and invasions of privacy. Further, Congress

---

[14] https://www.federalreserve.gov/releases/g19/current/
[15] 15 U.S.C. §1692 et seq.
[16] Section 802(a)

believes that the laws that existed prior to the FDCPA were inadequate to protect consumers, who deserved a private right of action to "police" these debt collection bullies. Accordingly, the purpose of the FDCPA is to "eliminate abusive debt collection practices by debt collectors, to ensure that those debt collectors who refrain from using abusive debt collection practices are not competitively disadvantaged, and to promote consistent state action to protect consumers against debt collection abuses."[17]

It is important to note two things about the FDCPA: (1) it applies only to consumer debts, so if you're being harassed by a bank for that business loan you took out, then the FDCPA will not protect you. (2) it applies only to the debt collection company, and not the lender itself, so if you're being chased by Visa® for a debt owed to Visa® then the FDCPA will not protect you.

---

[17] Section 802(e)

Although creditors have a "bona fide" error defense for innocent mistakes,[18] in most cases, the debt collector faces strict liability. In one case I handled, the debt collector was found liable for failing to provide a statement with their collection letter describing the borrower's rights under the FDCPA.

Although not an exhaustive list, the following constitute harassment and the creditor may face liability under the FDCPA:

- Confirm anything other than the location of the debtor if talking to anyone other than the debtor (like a family member or friend).[19]
- Communicating with the consumer if he is represented by an attorney.[20]
- Communicating with the consumer before 8 AM or after 9 PM local time.[21]

---

[18] Section 813(c)
[19] Section 804(1)
[20] Section 804(6) & Section 805(a)(2)
[21] Section 805(a)(1)

- Communicating with the consumer at work if the employer prohibits personal calls at the office.[22]
- Using or threatening violence.[23]
- Using obscene or profane language.[24]
- Calling repeatedly or continuously with the intent to annoy, abuse or harass.[25]
- Giving the false representation that the debt collector is affiliated with the United States, including the use of a badge or uniform.[26]
- The false representation of the character, amount or legal status of any debt.[27]
- Falsely representing that any communication is from an attorney.[28]

---

[22] Section 805(3)
[23] Section 806(1)
[24] Section 806(2)
[25] Section 806(5)
[26] Section 807(1)
[27] Section 807(2)
[28] Section 807(3)

- Falsely representing that failing to pay the debt will result in the consumer's arrest or imprisonment.[29]
- False documents intended to appear to be legal process (in other words, sending you documents that appear to be from the court but are not).[30]
- The false representation or deceptive means to collect or attempt to collect any debt or to obtain information concerning a consumer.[31]

Note that I just listed the highlights, the most common violations, rather than the complete list from the statute. If you feel like you're being bullied by a debt collector, please seek competent legal advice to determine if you have a cause of action against the debt collector for being too aggressive in their attempts to collect the debt (or the alleged debt) that you owe.

---

[29] Section 807(4)
[30] Section 807(13)
[31] Section 807(10)

One last thing about the FDCPA; although the debt collector faces strict liability, that liability is capped at $1,000.00 – not $1,000 per violation, but $1,000 total – plus any actual damages that can be proven, plus attorney's fees and court costs. Accordingly, when appropriate the FDCPA is paired with other causes of action to increase the damage award to the debtor in the event the debtor prevails.

In the event you're being harassed by the owner of the debt themselves, Florida has a companion consumer protection law called the Florida Consumer Collection Practices Act ("FCCPA").[32]

Like the FDCPA, the FCCPA prohibits:[33]

- Simulating a law enforcement officer or a representative of any governmental agency.
- Using or threatening force or violence.

---

[32] Florida Statute §559.55 et seq.
[33] Florida Statutes §559.72

- Communicating or threatening to communicate with a debtor's employer before obtaining final judgment against the debtor.
- Disclosing to a person other than the debtor or her or his family information affecting the debtor's reputation.
- Disclosing information concerning the existence of a debt known to be reasonably disputed by the debtor without disclosing that fact.
- Willfully communicating with the debtor or any member of her or his family with such frequency as can reasonably be expected to harass the debtor or her or his family, or willfully engaging in other conduct which can reasonably be expected to abuse or harass the debtor or any member of her or his family.
- Using profane, obscene, vulgar, or willfully abusive language.
- Claiming, attempting, or threatening to enforce a debt when such person knows that the debt is not legitimate.

- Using a communication that simulates in any manner legal or judicial process or that gives the appearance of being authorized, issued, or approved by a government, governmental agency, or attorney at law, when it is not.
- Communicating with a debtor under the guise of an attorney by using the stationery of an attorney or forms or instruments that only attorneys are authorized to prepare.
- Advertise or threaten to advertise for sale any debt to enforce payment.
- Publishing, posting, or threatening to publish or post before the public individual names or any list of names of debtors, commonly known as a deadbeat list.
- Refusing to provide adequate identification of herself or himself or her or his employer or other entity whom she or he represents if requested to do so by a debtor from whom she or he is collecting or attempting to collect a consumer debt.

- Mailing any communication to a debtor in an envelope or postcard with words typed, written, or printed on the outside of the envelope or postcard calculated to embarrass the debtor. An example of this would be an envelope addressed to "Deadbeat, Jane Doe" or "Deadbeat, John Doe."
- Communicating with the debtor between the hours of 9 p.m. and 8 a.m. in the debtor's time zone without the prior consent of the debtor.
- Communicating with a consumer if the person knows that the debtor is represented by an attorney with respect to such debt.

Just like the damages allowed by the FDCPA, the FCCPA will only allow $1,000 for the violation, regardless of how many violations, plus actual damages, attorney's fees and court costs.

What are "actual damages?" The best example I've heard (but never had the opportunity to raise in one of my cases) was a gentleman who, after being harassed repeatedly by telephone calls had a heart attack and was rushed to the hospital. The ambulance ride, emergency room bills, and doctor bills were all actual damages that were compensated by the creditor when sued under the FDCPA & FCCPA.

Recently, I used these two laws to the benefit of one of my clients. My client turned in a jet-ski to the creditor, who sold it at auction to pay the debt and then sued my client for the balance of the money owed. There were two problems: (1) the creditor never gave my client credit for the value of the jet ski received at auction (misrepresenting the amount of the debt owed) and, (2) the creditor was charging my client 24.99% interest instead of the contractual 22.99% interest (collecting money to which they were not entitled because of the exaggerated interest rate). I first tried negotiating with the creditor, which was politely refused. I then filed my answer and affirmative defenses, which were ignored. Finally, to get the creditor's attention, I filed a counter-claim in their collection lawsuit raising both the FDCPA and FCCPA claims. Shortly thereafter I was contacted by the creditor who asked if we could each drop our respective lawsuits! Poof! Approximately $21,000 of alleged debt owed was eliminated because the creditor was too aggressive in attempting to collect it from my client!

With the advent of cellular telephones, creditors have new opportunities and we have new challenges. Congress needed a mechanism to restrict or reduce the number of "robo-calls," especially in the early days of cell phone usage, when minute plans were the norm and most people paid per usage for their devices.

In 1991, Congress enacted the Telephone Consumer Protection Act ("TCPA").[34] The TCPA protects consumers who receive automated telemarketing calls, unsolicited faxes, or pre-recorded or automated calls to their cell phones.

---

[34] 47 U.S.C. §227

Like the FDCPA and FCCPA, the TCPA creates a private cause of action to allow consumers to police overly-abusive debt collectors who use automated systems to call your cell phone. Different from the FDCPA and FCCPA there is no attorney fee or cost provision (meaning you must pay your own attorney's fees and court costs) but the TCPA has teeth that its two cousins fail to have – the violations range from $500 to $1,500 *per phone call*!

My best success story with the TCPA is from 2012. The creditor made unsolicited, automated calls to my client before we got involved in the case. My firm sent a letter to the creditor asking them to stop calling our client and to deal with us directly. The client got nearly a hundred and seventy-five *more* calls even after the creditor received our letter. We settled with the creditor for $75,000: $25,000 of that paid off the debt owed to the creditor, and we split the remaining $50,000 with our client to cover attorney fees and court costs. When I first started to promote the TCPA as a consumer protection statute, I had clients change their ring tones to something to do with money and associate it to the creditor who was harassing them. Cha-ching!

How do you prove that the debt collector or creditor is being abusive? How do you prove that the calls are too frequent, before 8:00 AM or after 9:00 PM? I like to use a "Call Log." I ask my clients to keep a pad of paper near the phone and draw lines to create 5 columns. Then, every time they get a call write down: (1) the date, (2) the time, (3) the number, (4) the name of the person calling, and (5) the company they're calling from. Other clients have created narrative-format notes about what was discussed. Other clients have taken screenshots of their incoming and missed calls on their cell phone. Doing this at the time the call is received is great evidence to show a judge or jury when making your case against the abusive debt collector or harassing creditor.

If you want me to email you a call log, please email me at: Shawn@YesnerLaw.com, and include "Call Log" in the subject line.

Crushing Debt Tip

Keep records. Keep a call log. Generate as much information as possible to provide your attorney with the ammunition necessary to go on the offensive against overly-aggressive debt collection companies and creditors.

Chapter 4 - Foreclosure

Foreclosure law holds a special place in my heart (there, I said it).

When people learn I am an attorney, they want to know "Why did you choose real estate and bankruptcy law?" Truth be told, I wanted to be a tax attorney because my undergraduate degree is in accounting and I enjoy math and numbers, but my first job out of law school was with an attorney who focused on residential and commercial real estate closings. I once asked a friend of mine, now a well-respected family law attorney in Birmingham, Alabama, "Why would you want to do divorce law? How can you stand to see families torn apart?" His response was simple, "Who goes to see an attorney when something has gone right?" Real estate law was (at the time) one of the exceptions. I loved completing a closing and seeing the buyer walk out with what, to them, was a new house, and the seller walked away with a big fat check – an area of law where people go to see an attorney because something went right!

And, an area of law that has very little to do with being bullied! I'm in!

I later moved to Clearwater and took a job at what we now call a "foreclosure mill." I was exposed to all types of law centered around real estate: title issues, litigation, bankruptcy, landlord/tenant, appeals, and closings. I found the area of law to be fascinating and I became good at my job representing lenders – my fastest foreclosure was ninety-seven days from the time I filed the case until we had a foreclosure sale.

In 2004, my boss decided to shut down the mortgage foreclosure practice within her law firm, taking the firm from over a hundred and fifty people and twelve attorneys, down to two attorneys and two staff in about six months' time. I thought "What am I going to do so my own mortgage file doesn't come across my desk?" I was out of school for six years at the time and I knew a lateral move to another foreclosure mill would not give me any career satisfaction. I realized I knew how to complete foreclosures quickly, so the opposite could also work—being on the other side and trying to slow them down for consumers in danger of losing their homes. Plus, defending people in foreclosure fell more in line with my disdain for bullying. My career as a foreclosure defense attorney, real estate attorney, consumer protection attorney, creditor harassment attorney and bankruptcy attorney began in my living room at my house in Clearwater right around Thanksgiving 2004.

When clients come to see me today, one of their main concerns is "Will I come home tomorrow to find the bank has locked me out of my house?" Typically, the bank will give you about three months to catch up the mortgage before they decide to file a foreclosure lawsuit. So, the answer depends on where we are in the foreclosure process, which typically consists of the following events:

- Notice of Default and Acceleration. This is the letter that says, in essence "you are now ninety days or more behind and if you don't catch up immediately, we're going to try to collect the full balance of the loan that we gave you and repossess the house by filing a foreclosure lawsuit."

- Complaint and Lis Pendens. People think the Lis Pendens starts the foreclosure lawsuit and that is mostly true. The complaint starts the lawsuit. The lis pendens provides notice on the county public records that a lawsuit has been filed that may impact the property. A foreclosure lawsuit should always include a lis pendens, but a lis pendens does not always signify a foreclosure lawsuit. The lis pendens could indicate a quiet title lawsuit (asking the court to confirm someone's disputed ownership of a piece of property), partition (forcing the sale of property owned by people who are not married when they're unable to agree on what to do with the property), boundary dispute, insurance litigation, or other type of lawsuit that impacts the property.

- Service of Process. This is where the process server knocks on the door to hand you the foreclosure papers – they are not there to arrest you, even if the person who shows up is a sheriff, and you should accept the papers. If you choose to ignore the process server, you're just increasing your costs because the costs to the bank increase while they attempt to serve you, and you're simply kicking the can down the road, delaying the inevitable.

- Answer/Default. In Florida, you have twenty days to respond to a foreclosure lawsuit from the date of service of the lawsuit. Many times, we can extend this period by filing a motion with the judge and negotiating an extension with plaintiff's counsel. This alone is a good reason to get an attorney involved as early as possible.

- Mediation. Florida has adopted a process where we can ask the court to provide a mediator to try and modify the loan. To say the success rate of these mediations stink is to undervalue the word "stink." I think the success rate is a single-digit percentage (or lower) – let's just say that in my (now) seventeen years of practicing this area of law, I've had one mortgage foreclosure mediation where we got up from the table, shook hands and signed an agreement with the bank, and that case was with a credit union. The majority of these have gone so badly for the consumers that, I once had the bank's attorney say to me "The only point of a mediation is to see if the borrower submitted the proper documents for the bank to consider a loan modification." Huh? Look up the definition of "mediation" and see if you find anything resembling the opposing counsel's definition. However, even if the mediation doesn't result in an agreeable settlement, the process of the mediation extends your time in the house, giving us an opportunity to find an acceptable solution.

- Summary Judgment Hearing. Under Florida Rules of Civil Procedure, the lender must give twenty-five-days' notice prior to setting a hearing for final judgment (twenty days if by mail,[35] plus five extra days because of being sent by mail[36]). The standard to win at summary judgment is to prove that there is no issue of fact and the plaintiff is entitled to judgment as a matter of law.[37] Depending on the facts of your case, this could be an easy or difficult standard to overcome. The bank must give twenty-five days' notice to set the hearing, then find time on the judge's calendar (most of which are clogged

---

[35] Rule 1.510, Fla.R.Civ.P.

[36] Rule 1.090, Fla.R.Civ.P.

[37] Rule 1.510(c), Fla.R.Civ.P.

months out), then prove there is no issue of fact or issue of law.

- Trial. If summary judgment is denied (meaning the bank loses, not that the borrower wins), the bank will schedule a trial where all parties including the bank's representative, must appear to provide live, verbal testimony and evidence. Typically, the bank is going to win at this stage and a foreclosure sale will be scheduled. Florida law says the sale must be between twenty-eight and thirty-five days from the judgment date,[38] but we've been successful in getting sale dates sixty, ninety, one hundred and twenty, even one hundred and fifty days from the judgment date.

- Foreclosure Sale. Once the sale occurs, the Clerk of Court will not issue title to the successful bidder for ten days.[39] Once the buyer at the

---

[38] §45.031(1)(a), Fla.Stat. (2018)
[39] §45.031(5), Fla.Stat. (2018)

foreclosure sale gets title from the clerk of court, he can begin eviction proceedings, so even at the end, we're still not at the end ...

Using some of these delay tactics, we can typically, but not always, stretch a foreclosure out to a year or more in Florida. Of course, we don't do this simply to buy time, we have the homeowner/borrower working on a plan, whether that be a loan modification, Chapter 13 reorganization bankruptcy, short sale, Chapter 7 liquidation bankruptcy, deed in lieu of foreclosure, or some other alternative. Occasionally, we get a client with legitimate defenses and we can successfully defeat the bank in the foreclosure lawsuit because the bank's records were simply wrong. If we can get the court to rule in our favor, we then open the bank to liability under the FDCPA, FCCPA and potentially RESPA (Real Estate Settlement and Procedures Act).

I recall one case where we went to trial right before Christmas. I wanted the clients to know that the bank was not going to bully them out of their house for holidays. One of the bank's tactics was to request to postpone the trial so we could "work out a deal." While this would have postponed the case, it would have also left the clients in doubt as to whether they were going to lose their home, so we proceeded with trial. When the clients received the notice of default and acceleration, they called the bank to see if they could pay the balance to catch up the loan with money from their 401(k). The bank issued a new notice with an amount due through the end of the month. Around the middle of the month, the borrowers paid *more* than the amount owed to catch up the loan but paid it in two installments, about 40% of the amount owed in cash, and the rest by the 401(k) distribution check. The bank filed its foreclosure the next month! Then, the bank returned the money because: (1) they don't accept cash (huh?), and (2) they don't take reinstatement payments in installments. At trial, the judge (after a few choice words to the lender, including "why didn't you settle this case months ago?") ruled that the borrowers did properly reinstate the loan, and ruled in favor of the borrowers and against the mortgage company!

Of course, there are other attorneys that take the position that "all banks are evil," and "the default was caused by the bank, so it should not be allowed to foreclose." While there is some merit in that position, it typically only benefits the attorney, who has run up huge fees. This logic fails to fix the issue that caused payments to fall behind in the first place or fails to help the homeowner catch up payments.

Some of the more popular defenses these attorneys try to raise (at least the ones I know of at the time of writing this):

- Standing – does the bank have the right to bring the foreclosure action? Does it own and hold the note and mortgage? These days the answer is typically "yes," and the bank can prove it.

- Failure to Provide Notice – see step 1 in the section above. The bank must give a specific notice to the homeowner pursuant to the promissory note and mortgage contracts. If the bank fails to provide the correct notice, the basis of their foreclosure, a prerequisite of bringing the foreclosure lawsuit, is defective.

- Robo-Signing – the mortgage foreclosure defense "fad" of the late 2000's, largely done away with by bank procedures. Robo-signing is loosely defined as signing affidavits for the court case without reviewing the affidavits, or forging the signature of the signor or the notary. While improper, it is my opinion that robo-signing went to the sufficiency of the evidence (the robo-signed affidavit) and failed to address that in most cases, the borrower legitimately stopped making payments.

In the end, if the homeowner fell behind, they likely had a legitimate reason for doing so. That legitimate reason rarely rises to the level of a legal affirmative defense so we cannot use that to defeat the bank, we can simply use that defense to try to delay the bank's repossession. The borrower should seek out a local attorney to represent them in foreclosure in the event they do have a valid affirmative defense to the foreclosure lawsuit.

Crushing Debt Tip

The earlier the better. Most of the former techniques used to battle foreclosure cases are now gone by statute or case (judge-made) law. Like a criminal defense attorney, however, we can use the foreclosure laws to force the bank to prove their entitlement to foreclose, thus slowing down the process to help you come up with a solution to save or get rid of the house with minimal impact on your liability.

Chapter 5 - Loan Modification

The best options for a homeowner behind in payments who wants to keep his house are to reinstate the loan, refinance the loan, modify the loan, or file Chapter 13 reorganization.

Typically, reinstatement and refinance of the loan are difficult options. Reinstatement is when the homeowner simply pays whatever is owed to catch up the loan, in one lump sum (see the story at the end of the previous chapter). Reinstatement includes full payment of all past-due monthly payments, late charges, and fees and costs, including attorney fees, inspection fees, escrow fees, etc. For a loan with monthly payments of $1,000, a six-month payment arrears could result in a reinstatement of over $9,000 once all the fees and charges are factored into the loan. Similarly, refinance is typically too difficult an option because in most cases the house has insufficient equity to borrow against, and the homeowner's credit has been damaged by the reporting of late payments by the mortgage company.

Two other terms are also often referenced by clients, by the bank or by "internet lawyers," are forbearance and repayment. If affordable, go for the repayment, not the forbearance. A repayment plan takes the reinstatement amount and spreads it over some short-term period like twelve months, adding that amount to the mortgage payment, so that at the end of the repayment plan the loan is current. A forbearance plan is simply an agreement to pay the bank some monthly amount designed solely to avoid foreclosure – to have the bank "forbear" on its right to foreclose while you're making payments. The monthly payments do not reinstate the loan, they only keep the bank at bay, so when the forbearance is over, the homeowner could still face a foreclosure lawsuit or a continuation of the existing foreclosure lawsuit with no or little reduction in the balance owed to catch up the loan.

As I write this book, most of Florida is still recovering from Hurricane Irma. Most banks provided relief to homeowners impacted by

Irma by giving them three months of no payments (October, November & December 2017). Once 2018 started, however, it was time to pay the piper. Some banks allowed their homeowner/borrowers to modify their mortgages, wrapping the three months of non-payment back into the term of the loan. Other banks either required the homeowner/borrower to repay the three-months deficit in January, or simply considered the loan three months behind. We are just now seeing the impact of lenders who refused to work with homeowners after Hurricane Irma, arguing that their offer of a plan to make homeowner's budgets lighter for a few months, only to then foreclose on them later is improper. So far, no wins, but no losses either…

Loan modification could be a good solution if the homeowner has suffered a drop in income or an unexpected increase in expenses. In most cases, the bank will calculate 31% of the homeowner's income and compare that to the monthly mortgage payment. If the bank can, it will drop principal balance, reduce interest rates, re-amortize the loan, extend the loan term back out 30 or 40 years, or some other option that reduces the monthly payment down to 31% of the borrower's gross (before expenses) income. Note, if there is too big a gap between 31% of income and the borrower's pre-modification mortgage payment, or if 31% of the borrower's income is greater than the pre-modification mortgage payment, then a loan modification will usually be denied. We are also starting to see denials when the loan has gone unpaid for too long, typically more than twelve months of no payments to the bank.

I had a good friend of mine pass away (although I still question the definition of "good friend" because he was a fan, not a graduate, of the University of Miami, while I am an FSU alumnus and fan). My friend passed when he was in his early thirties, leaving behind a wife, three minor children, a $10,000 life insurance policy and a house with a mortgage. His wife suddenly had a major drop in income, without him there. The problem we encountered in trying to modify the loan was that the promissory note was only in the name of my deceased friend, but the house was in the name of his wife; because the house was owned as Tenancy by the Entireties, 100% of the title to the house transferred to his widow by operation of law when he died. The bank refused to talk to us about the house because the borrower was not around to give authorization to speak to the wife (duh!). Therefore, we first had to file a probate, for no other reason than to get an order from the probate court allowing the wife to talk to the bank. Once we got that order, we were able to help the wife modify the loan and save the house. The best part, when the bank sent the modification papers, they indicated the borrower as "The Estate of ..." so even after the modification (likely a mistake by the bank that I am unable to explain), if the house remains underwater, the wife can simply walk away, with no negative impact to her liability or her credit.

In some instances, Chapter 13 reorganization is a great option to help families keep their homes. Chapter 13 cases can eliminate (or "strip") completely underwater second mortgages, association liens, and judgment liens, which are completely underwater if the amount owed on the first mortgage is greater than the value of the house. Chapter 13 can also consolidate and reduce payments to credit cards, hospital or medical bills, the IRS, and student loans. This frees up more income to catch up the mortgage payments over the sixty-month term of the bankruptcy plan. In addition, modification and Chapter 13 can be combined so that in addition to all the other benefits of the bankruptcy, the mortgage payment can be reduced by a modification of the loan as part of the Chapter 13 process.

One of the first questions that we ask a potential client is "What is your goal: to keep or sell the property?" We will then analyze all the available options and together, pick the option that is best for the client and his or her family.

However, loan modifications are not required by law, nor can a judge force the bank to modify the loan (except in limited, rare circumstances). Many times, the documentation requirements on homeowners can be extreme, and for some unknown reason, the banks never get the full package on the first try, requiring the borrower to send the voluminous loan mod package multiple times. Frustrated borrowers can choose to refuse to give documents for the umpteenth time to the lender. Accordingly, lenders can choose to decline loan modifications based on an alleged lack of documents submitted by the borrower.

People who refuse to provide documents to the bank fall into one of three categories:(1) unable to provide documents because the documents do not exist – these are people who keep poor records, (2) unable to provide documents because they are stubborn – these are the people who claim "the bank received a bailout, why not me too?!", or (3) unable to provide documents because they are hiding something – these borrowers don't want the lenders to see that they make hundreds of thousands a year in income, or just received a large inheritance or lottery winnings, for example.

Put simply, there is no federal or Florida Law that requires a mortgage company to modify a home mortgage. Consistent with what I said in Chapter 1, if you have the hand, show it to the bank because that's the best way to qualify for a loan modification.

Finally, the bank is going to want the homeowner to explain their "hardship." Frankly, I don't think the bank's employees read these, but they require hardship letters so they can keep the regulators happy. In our experience, some hardships will be easier to prove for a modification, including, but not limited to, death or disability of a co-borrower, divorce, loss of job or decrease in hours, a major medical issue, and military deployment.

Voluntary decisions are typically unacceptable as hardships, like the decision to have kids, thus increasing expenses. Years ago, at the beginning of the Great Recession,

I was on a panel discussion with a representative from Wells Fargo (I have a particular disdain for Wells Fargo, so I don't mind mentioning that bank specifically, despite my disclaimer at the beginning of the book). At that point, I was a newlywed but still had no kids. I lived in a two-bedroom, two-bathroom, one-car garage house that was just over 1,100 square feet. I asked the Wells Fargo rep who was also on the panel "Would it be a hardship if my wife got pregnant with triplets? Does the bank really expect five people, including three infants, to live in a two-bedroom 1,100-square foot house?". Wells Fargo's response was "That is not a hardship, because the decision to have kids is voluntary."

Most borrowers will say, "My house dropped in value and so I've lost a lot of money!" This is not a hardship. First, you haven't lost money until you try to sell the house for a lower price. Until that point, the loss is a "paper-loss" and unless the property is investment or rental property the loss will never result in less dollars in your pocket while the house is owned. Second, to the extent the house has lost value for the homeowner, it has also lost value for the bank. Therefore, the bank has a "hardship" equal to the mortgagor's hardship; they've both lost value in the secured asset. Unfortunately, a drop in value of the house is not a hardship for purposes of convincing the lender to give you a loan modification.

Obviously, there are more hardships available to borrowers considering a short sale or loan modification. If you want a copy of my template hardship letter, please email me at Shawn@YesnerLaw.com with the subject line "Hardship Letter." We are willing to be creative in the hardship we describe to the bank, so long as our representations to the bank are truthful rather than misleading.

Crushing Debt Tip

Loan modifications are great tools to reduce your monthly mortgage payment but are MOST effective when you have a long-term goal to remain in the house.

Chapter 6 - Short Sales

When facing a mortgage foreclosure, or even the possibility of a mortgage foreclosure, borrowers should ask: "What options are best for me and my family?" In the previous chapter, I described that I ask all my clients and potential clients: "What is your goal, to keep or sell the home?" If the borrower replies that they're intending to be removed by the coroner after living a long and fruitful life, the loan modification is the better solution. However, if the borrower says they're going to be empty nesters in three years after the last kid moves on to college, and they then want to downsize; or the opposite, that they just got married and they're planning on a larger house soon so they can start having kids, then let's short sale now rather than kicking the can down the road.

We can use one of three and a half options to help the homeowner who wants to part with the house: Short Sale, Deed in Lieu of Foreclosure, or Foreclosure, and Bankruptcy as a "half-option."

A short sale is when the borrower sells the home at a price that is at or near fair market value but is below the amount necessary to pay off the mortgage(s) in full and any lien(s) recorded against the property. Although in some cases, the homeowner must pay unpaid association assessments and property taxes, in most cases the homeowner will bring no money to closing. Any closing costs are absorbed by the purchase price of the property, and any deficiency is normally waived by the lender. Note that credit unions never, in our experience, waive deficiency but lenders will waive deficiency a great majority of the time, creating potential income tax issues. However, the possible income tax consequences oftentimes are outweighed by the sale of the house, lifting that financial burden from the homeowner.

When a debt is forgiven or waived by the bank, they send a notice of that waiver to the IRS; the notice is a 1099c. The IRS considers a 1099c to be a benefit to you because you do not have to repay the debt to the lender.

Anytime you get a benefit, Uncle Sam wants his cut. However, there are ways to reduce or eliminate the income tax owed because of a 1099c and you should consult a CPA or your tax preparer to see if you have to pay tax should you receive a 1099c.

Even with the potential tax consequences, a short sale may be in the homeowner's best interest. I have helped countless homeowners short sell their homes. However, it is not a decision to be taken lightly. I recall a conversation with a homeowner shortly after the Great Recession started. The homeowner was bragging that he was going to sell his home because it was "underwater." When I questioned the homeowner further, he said he had no intention of moving, but wanted to sell his house before he lost any more equity. That decision, at the time, seemed silly to me because the homeowner wanted to stay in the house and had a fixed-rate mortgage that was fully amortizing, meaning it would be paid to zero if he made his payments every month during the term of the mortgage. In other words, with his type of mortgage, regardless of the value of the house, the homeowner would have paid his mortgage down to $0.00, or at least paid it down enough that eventually the value would have been more than what was owed on the house. As I write this, most economists agree that we are out of the Great Recession and home values are increasing. That homeowner I spoke with years ago, would likely have equity in his home, and lots of it, had he stuck with the house and the monthly payments when we first spoke.

At the same time, I can think of countless clients where a short sale was a great idea:

- Negative equity of $100,000 or more (meaning that the house was worth $100,000 or more less than what the client owed to the bank);
- The client needed to move and was unwilling or unable to be a long-distance landlord, or rents dropped to the point where rent would not have covered the mortgage payment;
- Loss of job;
- Divorce;

- Medical hardship;
- Multiple mortgages against the property; and
- All of the other reasons why people want to or decide to move.

A deed in lieu of foreclosure, or "DIL," is a solution where the homeowner voluntarily gives the house back to the lender, if the lender will let them, in exchange for a waiver of the debt. The issue with a DIL is that before the bank takes back the property voluntarily, they want to ensure that the homeowner is unable to sell it at fair market value. Therefore, in most cases, before the lender will allow the DIL, the property must be listed with a licensed realtor, at fair market value or at the lender's pre-determined price for ninety days or more with no activity (although check with your lender because the specific requirements may differ depending on the lender.) The consequences of a DIL are the same as a short sale: the lender typically waives deficiency, which then requires the homeowner to do a tax analysis based on the "benefit" of the forgiven debt.

Many clients are confused about this point and want to jump right to the DIL, skipping the short sale. So far, I've had one bank contact me about doing a DIL without first trying to short sale the property – that's one bank in nearly seventeen years practicing in this area of law. Certainly, private individuals who hold notes and mortgage can decide to jump right to this step (and many have) but your traditional lenders typically want the house listed for sale first because, contrary to popular opinion, they are in the business of loaning money rather than managing houses.

A foreclosure is an option the bank chooses because the borrower chooses to do nothing. For a homeowner to say, "I'm going to choose to do a foreclosure" is really a statement by the homeowner that "I'm going to do nothing." There are some instances where allowing a property to be foreclosed is a good option. Typically, however, it is an option of last resort because while the consequences are mostly the same (waiver of deficiency) the impact to credit can be devastating following the completion of a foreclosure by the bank.

Finally, bankruptcy may help in the decision-making process but, under Florida law, the bankruptcy itself has no ability to convey title to the property. Sometimes the trustee will sell the house in bankruptcy otherwise, the homeowner must sell the house in a short sale, give it back in a deed in lieu, or foreclose as described in this chapter. Where a bankruptcy is a good option, and the trustee does not sell the house, we pair this solution with one of the other three - short sale, DIL or "do nothing" foreclosure.

Crushing Debt Tip

If the house is upside down (worth less than what is owed to the bank), and you want to get rid of the house, a majority of the time a short sale is going to be your best solution and allow you the fastest path towards recovery (financially and from a credit perspective).

Chapter 7 – Bankruptcy

While I'm going to devote an entire chapter to the subject of bankruptcy, understand that there are whole books devoted to the subject (maybe my second book will be such an undertaking?). While I've said it repeatedly, you should consult a local bankruptcy attorney if you believe bankruptcy is an applicable option to eliminate your debt.

The determination on whether to file bankruptcy, and then what chapter of bankruptcy – Chapter 7 (liquidation) or Chapter 13 (reorganization) – is largely based upon an analysis of the your income and non-exempt assets.

Bankruptcy may be a good choice in the following circumstances:

- You are unable to repay the debt, or the debtor has an inability to catch up that debt over a short period of time;
- You are facing foreclosure;
- You are facing a wage garnishment;

- You are facing a repossession of assets;
- You have huge medical bills (unless those bills are related to a personal injury case); or
- You were laid off and are either unable to find a new job or found a new job at a lower salary.

On the other hand, bankruptcy might be a bad choice in the following circumstances:

- You own 100% of a business that is valuable or profitable;
- You own some other expensive asset (like jewelry, multiple cars, multiple investment properties, etc.);
- You are entitled to a personal injury judgment;
- You are entitled to a large inheritance;
- Your debts may be non-dischargeable – related to the commission of a crime, some tortious act like theft, vandalism, fraud, etc., or maybe a tax obligation; or

- Some other method to eliminate the debt is appropriate.

In situations where bankruptcy is a bad option, we can explore other means of resolving outstanding debt with the creditors – like debt settlement, a negotiated drop in interest rates, a negotiated payment plan, or some other option. Maybe the borrower is "judgment proof" and has a "thick skin" where doing nothing is also an appropriate option.

Once you've made the decision to file, we must determine what chapter of bankruptcy is appropriate.

The first step in the analysis is the means test, which calculates the debtor's gross annual income based on a projection using the past six months of income. We then compare the debtor's gross annual income to the median income as determined by the IRS based upon how many people live in the home. If the annual income is less than median income, the debtor qualifies for Chapter 7 (liquidation). If the income is more than median income, the debtor can then deduct a combination of IRS and actual expenses to determine disposable income. If disposable income is negative or break-even, the debtor can still file Chapter 7. If disposable income is positive, the debtor may have to file Chapter 13 (reorganization).

The means test is complex and calculating median income or disposable income under the means test is somewhat of an art form. In addition, the means test is still relatively new, having been implemented in 2005, so there is still case law developing which may impact the means test. In addition, most Chapter 13 trustees consider the Chapter 13 itself to be a fluid thing, versus a Chapter 7 which is a snapshot in time. Therefore, as income increases or decreases, the debtor's Chapter 13 payment may change (up or down) consistent with their increase or decrease in income and expenses.

Often, I'm asked "my spouse makes no money, but I make a ton of money. Can my spouse file Chapter 7 alone?" Unfortunately, the answer may be "no." Early in my career, I assisted a Realtor® with a bankruptcy filing. My client made no money. His husband, on the other hand, had a salary that exceed six figures! The United States Trustee challenged the bankruptcy filing because bankruptcy is based on "household income" and between them, my client and his husband had income exceeding $150,000 – too much money for the one spouse to file alone. The logic of the US Trustee is that the spouse making the good salary would never allow the filing spouse to go without electricity, a roof over his head, food, etc.

Similarly, I helped another debtor with an aggressive Chapter 13 strategy. The situation was like the one above – the wife made no money and the husband made over six figures. The problem is that the wife was previously married, and her ex-husband kept the house. Both my client and her ex-husband remained liable for the note and mortgage. Unfortunately, years after the divorce the ex-husband passed away and therefore stopped making mortgage payments. The bank filed a foreclosure against the ex-husband's estate and my client. While a Chapter 7 would have been perfect to eliminate the mortgage debt on a house she no longer owned, the household income including her new husband far exceeded the threshold necessary to file a Chapter 7. Therefore, we filed a Chapter 13 for the wife alone. The reason this strategy is aggressive is because if the mortgage company filed a claim to be repaid its deficit, the Chapter 13 payments would have sky-rocketed. However, in any Chapter 13 case, only creditors who file claims can be paid. We surrendered the house to the bank in the Chapter 13 plan and the mortgage company failed to file a claim. We had one creditor – a credit card owed about $400 – make the singular claim in the bankruptcy case. The husband paid that claim, plus some administrative expenses, about $2,000 total, and all the wife's other debts, including that mortgage with her ex-husband, were eliminated!

There is no need to feel ashamed or embarrassed by your decision to protect yourself and your family. All good bankruptcy attorneys will tell you that you are simply using the law as it was designed, as a tool to eliminate debt and get your financial house in order.

Interestingly, the bankruptcy code was amended in 2005, by the Bankruptcy Abuse Prevention and Consumer Protection Act ("BAPCPA"). This amendment was largely in response to a perception in Congress that the "stigma" of filing bankruptcy has decreased over the four decades between the creation of the bankruptcy code that we know today (the Bankruptcy Reform Act of 1978) and the late-1990's and early 2000's. An article entitled The Persistence of Bankruptcy Stigma written by Associate Professor of Law Michael D. Sousa for the *American Bankruptcy Institute Law Review*[40] suggests that the stigma of filing bankruptcy has actually increased over the previous four decades and that BAPCPA is founded on an incorrect premise of

---

[40] *American Bankruptcy Institute Law Review*, The Persistence of Bankruptcy Stigma, Page 217, Vol 26, Num 2, Summer 2018

decreasing stigma surrounding the filing of bankruptcy.

Regardless, the perception or stigma is just that, intangible. There is no tangible mark to show who has filed a bankruptcy case. While the filing may be public record, the information is not readily available through an internet search, like state court data on lawsuits filed by or against you.

One you determine that bankruptcy is the best option, you must calculate actual income — income less expenses. Again, if you are negative or break-even at the end of the month, you can file Chapter 7. If you have positive or disposable income, then you might have to file Chapter 13.

Finally, you need to review any assets that have high dollar value, such as jewelry, businesses, cars that are paid off, personal injury lawsuits or inheritances, investment and vacation homes. Some assets of high value (IRA, 401k) are exempt and these can be ignored for this part of the analysis. In

Florida, the debtor will normally be able to exempt $1,000 of the value of a car[41], and $1,000 of anything else (or $5,000 of anything else if the debtor rents rather than owns his home[42]). Therefore, a debtor with a $4,000 car free and clear of debt, and a business worth $10,000 will, at best, be able to protect $6,000 in value, leaving $8,000 ($4,000 + $10,000 - $1,000 - $5,000) to be liquidated and paid to unsecured creditors. If the debtor can pay $8,000 to the trustee, Chapter 7 is an option (which is why this type of bankruptcy is called liquidation). If the debtor is unable to pay a lump sum of $8,000 to the trustee, then Chapter 13 is the better option because the $8,000 can be paid over a maximum of sixty months, generating payments of approximately $133.33 ($8,000 / 60 months). The trustee then disburses the $8,000 to creditors (after deducting the trustee's administrative fees of course).

In bankruptcy consultations, we are often asked "What can I do to qualify for

---

[41] §222.25(1)
[42] §222.25(4)

bankruptcy?" or "look better" for bankruptcy, or the related question, "Should I quit my job, get a divorce, incur more debt, etc. to be able to file bankruptcy?"

My first full year as a solo practitioner was 2005. The firm did well, and I was able to make a good salary as a single guy with little debt and less responsibility. I mentioned to my father, who is a CPA, that I was worried about the amount of taxes I would have to pay based on a salary that, at that time, was the most I had ever made at that point in my life. I could feel my father's urge to reach through the phone and smack me upside the head. "Why would you want to make less money?" he asked, while audibly grinding his teeth in frustration. "You'll be able to pay the taxes if you're making good money." That lesson has stuck with me and applies to my clients also. We counsel our clients to avoid confusing the income issues in bankruptcy by trying to determine "How much do I have to make to look like I can file bankruptcy?" Our advice to clients is for them to make as much money as they can and let me help them handle disclosure of their income.

In addition, debtors and their counsel have a duty of honesty to the bankruptcy court and bankruptcy trustee. The bankruptcy petition is signed under oath under penalty of perjury, so doing things like intentionally cutting hours, quitting, getting a divorce, etc., could expose you to criminal liability for perjury, which is much worse than a bankruptcy. I would be more worried about a knock at the door from the FBI (who investigates bankruptcy crimes) than service of process by a creditor trying to collect money.

Therefore, we advise clients to be an open book to the bankruptcy court and trustee; hide nothing. There will be obvious red flags that the court and trustee will see when a debtor cuts hours intentionally, quits their job, gets a divorce, etc. Plus, the bankruptcy trustees and judges handle thousands of cases each year – they've see every situation, and have a general distrust of debtors, so why tempt that they're going to take a closer look at your case by trying to fudge the numbers to look better in bankruptcy court? Both the trustee and I have years of experience in bankruptcy court, it is very rare or impossible for you to be smarter than the bankruptcy code to think of some strategy that will allow you to stretch the truth to the point of dishonesty.

Further, for the debtor who wants to intentionally cut their hours or quit their job, why? Typically, we tell clients to make as much money as they can and it's our job to use the data to advise on the possibility of bankruptcy versus another debt settlement option.

With the divorce question specifically, we believe that you don't get married for money, so don't get divorced for money either. Plus, to "sell" the trustee on the financial hardship because of the divorce or separation the loving couple will now have to pick up an additional rent payment, utility bills, moving expenses, and other factors related to running two separate households.

Advising a client to incur more debt is specifically prohibited by the Bankruptcy Code, so as attorneys we are unable to ethically and legally provide that type of advice. Sometimes, I am asked whether the debtor can buy a new car just prior to filing. If you need a new car, then go for it. While the means test allows an expense more than $500 for a car loan (even if your monthly payment is $300, you still get a deduction of around $500 on the means test) I am unable to advise you to take on debt to make your means test numbers "better." However, if you need a new car, then buy a new car. Just don't trade in your Toyota Camry for a Cadillac, or your Honda Civic for a Porsche!

Sometimes, we get the related "how much debt do I need to have to be able to file bankruptcy?" The answer is easy: there is no threshold amount of debt necessary to file bankruptcy. In our opinion, you need only have more debt than you can afford to repay. For example, $10,000 of debt to someone who makes $100,000 per year is manageable, but devastating to someone who makes $40,000 a year, and not even on the radar to someone who makes $1,000,000 per year.

Often, the decision to file comes down to the individual. Some people believe that if they borrowed the money, they have a moral obligation to repay the money. Other people have no issue with discharging debt to a major credit card company, knowing that company is going to continue making a profit despite the discharge of whatever you owe them.

Crushing Debt Tip

Bankruptcy is a great tool to eliminate or restructure debt that is burdensome. While some people understandably have moral issues with filing a bankruptcy, it is NOT a four-letter word and it is something that, in the long term, has very little impact on your life. Collect all your income and expense information, and any information related to the value of your assets, then meet with an experienced attorney to determine whether bankruptcy is a good option for you.

Chapter 8 - Student Loans

Since high school, I knew that I wanted to be an attorney. As I write this, I have been out of law school for twenty years, I'm approaching twenty years since I passed the Florida Bar and became an attorney, and still have another ten years before my student loans are paid off; making my student loans on par with a home loan. The one difference is that there is no collateral for my student loan. It is not like my student loan lenders can repossess the knowledge that I've gained during college, law school and beyond. They can't repossess my brain (at least I don't think they can). What happens, however, if I am unable to pay back my student loans? Many former students face this question every day, and, unfortunately, more will face this question moving forward.

The bankruptcy code, section 523(a)(8) prohibits Federal student loans from being discharged in bankruptcy. Similarly, private loans issued by for-profit companies for any educational benefit are exempt from discharge under section 523(a)(8)(B). Congress intended to make student loans difficult to discharge because at the time of graduation the graduate's salary is at its lowest point, and the student loan debt is at its highest point. Although there is little empirical data to back up the analysis, Congress believes that the stigma of filing bankruptcy, and the other tests built into the bankruptcy code are not stringent enough to prevent savvy graduates from running up student loan debt and filing bankruptcy just after crossing the stage to pick up their diploma. Of course, I believe that Congress is disconnected from the cost of obtaining an education (I believe Congress is disconnected from their constituents in general, but I digress), and schools have increased tuition beyond the rate of inflation, thus devaluing a degree from what it was worth even a few years ago.

As with any rule, however, there are exceptions. Student loans can be discharged if the debtor can prove that repayment of the loan would subject the borrower to "undue hardship," an undefined term, thus open to court interpretation: The "Johnson" test[43] examines the debtor's past finances and likely future finances, the debtor's good faith efforts to pay off the loan, and the debtor's motive in filing bankruptcy. The "Bryant"[44] test is objective, finding undue hardship when the debtor's "after-tax net income is below Federal poverty guidelines. Some courts use the "Totality of the Circumstances" Test examining all the circumstances surrounding the financial situation of the debtor including their financial resources, necessary expenses, and any other relevant factors. Finally, most courts require the bankruptcy filer to prove: (a) an inability to maintain a minimal standard of living if forced to repay the loans; (b) whether any additional circumstances exist that show that the debtor's state of affairs is likely to persist for a significant portion of the repayment period; and (c) that there have been good faith efforts to repay the student loan(s).

---

[43] *In re: Johnson*, No. 77-2033 TT, 1979 U.S. Dist. LEXIS 11428, at *20 (Bankr. E.D. Pa. 1979).
[44] *Bryant v. Pennsylvania Higher Educ. Assistance Agency (In re Bryant)*, 72 B.R. 913 (Bankr. E.D. Pa. 1987)

Proving undue hardship is extremely difficult. Undue hardship means more than temporary or even severe financial difficulty. Debtors must establish that it will never be possible for them to pay off their student loans under any foreseeable or unforeseeable circumstance. In some cases, the debtor must have a serious and permanent medical condition or disability that arose after incurring the student loans (from an accident, for example). In addition, discharge has been allowed in some cases where the debtor had extended periods of homelessness and an inability to find or maintain a place to live. The Middle District of Florida has adopted the three-part Brunner Test[45] used by most of the country, although some judges have applied an additional factor - whether the debtor has tried to minimize monthly expenses.

What is the solution, outside of Congress amending the bankruptcy code? Federal student loans can be deferred or put into

---

[45] *Brunner v. New York State Higher Education Services Corp.*, 831 F.2d 395 (2d Cir. 1987)

payment plans. If the student loan companies refuse to defer the debt, Chapter 13 might still be an option. Although not dischargeable, student loans are not priority debts either - meaning they are paid like other general unsecured debts. Thus, if the reorganization plan proposes to pay 25% to all unsecured creditors, then the student loan company will get 25% of what it is owed during the five-year (sixty-month) term of the Chapter 13 plan and, at the end of five years, the remaining 75% would be owed, which can be renegotiated with the student loan company.

While we are still keeping a close eye on developments in bankruptcy court and other areas to help our clients eliminate student loan debt, one resolution that may be of tremendous benefit is to consolidate your student loans. One of the best programs we've seen is the William D. Ford Direct Loan Consolidation Program.

Consolidation of student loans provides a great benefit in that it takes many loans and combines them into one payment with one interest rate, with one lender. Also, in some situations, consolidation under the Ford program may reduce your monthly payment to $0, temporarily, while still reporting your loan payment status as current. Loan repayment is based on income and the ability to repay meaning the repayment amount is flexible year to year. Also, under the Ford program, loans are forgiven after twenty to twenty-five years of on time payments (including payments of $0.00). That means that if there is any balance left over after twenty to twenty-five years, depending on your specific program, that balance is waived.

However, there are some drawbacks to consider as well. If your loan repayment term before consolidation is less than –twenty to twenty-five years, consolidation under the Ford program will extend the repayment term. Also, if you have negotiated favorable terms with your student loan company, those terms will be lost in consolidation (although, hopefully, replaced with more favorable terms under the Ford program).

The following student loans are eligible for this program:

- Direct Subsidized
- Direct Unsubsidized
- Federal Perkins Loans
- Parent Plus Loans
- Stafford Unsubsidized
- Stafford Subsidized
- Supplemental Loans for Students (SLS)
- Federal Nursing Loans
- Health Education Assistance Loans
- FFEL Loans (must be consolidated with another loan, or applying for PSLF)

We will continue to monitor legal developments in the student loan realm. Please subscribe to The Crushing Debt Podcast and visit our blog at www.yesnerlaw.com for more details.

Crushing Debt Tip

As of the drafting of this book, student loan debts are non-dischargeable in bankruptcy court. However, we have multiple tools at our disposal to make student loan payments bearable. Before choosing an option to help manage your student loan payments, get educated about the type of student loan you have, and what options are available – including forbearance plans, repayment plans, consolidation plans and, in certain extreme cases, bankruptcy.

Chapter 9 – IRS

When I meet with a client who owes money to the IRS, we determine whether the IRS has filed a lien against real property or if the IRS is trying to collect a debt owed by the client, or both.

Despite contrary language in the Florida constitution[46], federal tax liens can be enforced against homestead property[47]. To levy against the taxpayer's homestead, the IRS must be owed more than $5,000[48], and the IRS must obtain a court order from a judge or magistrate of the United States District Court[49]. In practice, I've never seen the IRS try to foreclose a taxpayer's primary residence, probably because money (tax refunds, bank accounts, etc.) is an easier target. Also, in foreclosure cases I've handled, both for the lender and the homeowner, the IRS lien is second in priority to a purchase

---

[46] Florida Constitution, Article X, Section 4
[47] 26 U.S. Code §6334
[48] 26 U.S. Code §6334(a)(13)(A)
[49] 26 U.S. Code §6334(e)

money mortgage. In other words, if the homeowner uses the funds from the lender to buy the house, then the IRS is second in line to that first mortgage. The IRS is superior to a second mortgage, and a mortgage used to refinance the property to get cash out of the house, which is why the IRS will need to be paid before or as part of a closing for a second mortgage, HELOC (Home Equity Line of Credit) or cash-out refinance.

Finally, the United States Supreme Court ruled that the IRS can enforce a federal tax lien against property owned by a husband and wife, even when the lien is against one spouse alone, eliminating the tenancy by the entireties protection provided by Florida law.[50]

What happens when you're trying to sell a house with a recorded federal tax lien? Use IRS Form 14135, Application for Certificate of Discharge of Property from a Federal Tax Lien.[51] It's a straightforward form, about four

---

[50] *United States v. Craft*, 535 U.S. 274 (2002)
[51] www.IRS.gov

or five pages long, which requires the taxpayer to provide information and attached supporting information like the settlement statement or closing disclosure, the contract, property values, appraisals, copies of the other liens that are involved, title searches, etc.

The packages that I've submitted have been forty to fifty pages each with all the supporting documents. The purpose of the application is to ask the IRS to do one of two things: (1) release the lien against the house because there is no equity available for the IRS after payment of the first mortgage and closing costs, or (2) allow the closing and whatever is left is paid to the IRS to release its lien. Note that in both of these cases, the taxpayer is not asking the IRS to eliminate the debt owed, just to relieve the house of the burden of the tax lien. I've done both types of applications and negotiated with the IRS. The negotiations were difficult, but they worked in each case. We got a release that the title company recorded, we closed, and the IRS was paid (or not), consistent with the IRS's instructions. In a few cases, the IRS demanded more than what we had in proceeds after deducting the first mortgage and closing costs; in each of those cases, the taxpayer paid the balance to proceed with the closing.

What happens when the IRS is trying to collect a debt from the taxpayer – we negotiate with the IRS of course! Whether we're dealing with the IRS or a credit card company or collection agency, we can still negotiate – with the IRS, this is called an offer in compromise.

As defined by the IRS, "An offer in compromise (OIC) is an agreement between a taxpayer and the Internal Revenue Service that settles a taxpayer's tax liabilities for less than the full amount owed."[52]

To qualify for an OIC, the taxpayer must have: (1) filed all tax returns, (2) made all required estimated tax payments for the current year, (3) made all required federal tax deposits for the current quarter if the taxpayer is an employer business owner.

---

[52] https://www.irs.gov/taxtopics/tc204

The IRS might accept an OIC on one of three grounds: (1) if there is doubt or dispute as to the existence of the debt or the amount owed, (2) if there is doubt as to the collectability of the taxpayer (see Chapter 1), or (3) requiring payment in full would create an economic hardship on the taxpayer or would be unfair because of exceptional circumstances.

To determine if you qualify for an OIC, and to submit the application to the IRS, I suggest you seek out a local tax attorney or CPA. As with the means test in bankruptcy, there is an art to completing an application for an OIC.

If you are unable to negotiate or qualify for an OIC, you may consider bankruptcy to eliminate your tax obligations. However, in most cases, IRS debt is non-dischargeable[53] (meaning unaffected by the bankruptcy case, other than the automatic stay which delays collection of the debt temporarily). A Chapter 13 (reorganization) may help in that it allows the debtor/taxpayer to repay the IRS over the

---

[53] 11 U.S. Code §523(a)(1)

life of the bankruptcy plan, which is sixty months – five years – in most cases.

If the taxpayer/debtor qualifies, the Chapter 7 (liquidation) might discharge the tax debt if:

- The taxes owed are income taxes;
- The taxpayer did not commit fraud or willful tax evasion;
- The income tax debt is more than three (3) years' old;
- The tax return for the year owed was filed at least two (2) years before filing the bankruptcy case; and
- The income tax debt was assessed by the IRS at least 240 days before the bankruptcy was filed.

Note that this analysis fails (and the debt will be non-dischargeable) if, for example, the income tax debt is for the 2015 tax year, but as of 2018, returns have not been filed – failing the last point that the debt must be assessed more than two hundred and forty days before the bankruptcy is filed, and the fourth point that the return was filed more than two years' prior to the bankruptcy filing.

Like the OIC, please consult a local attorney, CPA, or enrolled agent to determine whether the tax debt is dischargeable prior to filing your bankruptcy case. It would be awful to file bankruptcy just to discharge income tax obligations, only to learn you don't qualify to discharge the tax!

Crushing Debt Tip

The biggest mistake we see clients make is a complete failure to file tax returns. Filing a return, even when money is owed, will start the statute of limitations clock, and may start the taxpayer on the path to dischargeability if he ever needs to file bankruptcy. Plus, as with other sections of this book, keep and retain documents to refer to years later if necessary.

Full List of Crushing Debt Tips:

Chapter 1 - Debt Settlement, it Ain't Poker

In most cases, full disclosure is a more effective technique than withholding information. When the creditor knows you have nothing to give, that there is no pot of gold at the end of your rainbow, they will likely leave you alone, or set themselves up to be sued for over-aggressive debt collection practices.

Chapter 2 - Dealing with Zombie Debt

Keep track of all of your old debts that are written off, paid off, discharged in bankruptcy, too old, or eliminated in some other way. If they come back to life, if a creditor contacts you to collect that money, there are some great tools to erase this Zombie Debt!

Chapter 3 - Keep your Call Log

Keep records. Keep a call log. Generate as much information as possible to provide your attorney with the ammunition necessary to go on the offensive against overly-aggressive debt collection companies and creditors.

Chapter 4 - Foreclosure

The earlier the better. Most of the former techniques used to battle foreclosure cases are now gone by statute or case (judge-made) law. Like a criminal defense attorney, however, we can use the foreclosure laws to force the bank to prove their entitlement to foreclose, thus slowing down the process to help you come up with a solution to save or get rid of the house with minimal impact on your liability.

Chapter 5 - Loan Modification

Loan modifications are great tools to reduce your monthly mortgage payment but are MOST effective when you have a long-term goal to remain in the house.

Chapter 6 - Short Sales

If the house is upside down (worth less than what is owed to the bank), and you want to get rid of the house, a majority of the time a short sale is going to be your best solution and allow you the fastest path towards recovery (financially and from a credit perspective).

Chapter 7 - Bankruptcy

Bankruptcy is a great tool to eliminate or restructure debt that is burdensome. While some people understandably have moral issues with filing a bankruptcy, it is NOT a four-letter word and it is something that, in the long term, has very little impact on your life. Collect all your income and expense information, and any information related to the value of your assets, then meet with an experienced attorney to determine whether bankruptcy is a good option for you.

Chapter 8 - Student Loans

As of the drafting of this book, student loan debts are non-dischargeable in bankruptcy court. However, we have multiple tools at our disposal to make student loan payments bearable. Before choosing an option to help manage your student loan payments, get educated about the type of student loan you have, and what options are available – including forbearance plans, repayment plans, consolidation plans and, in certain extreme cases, bankruptcy.

Chapter 9 – IRS

The biggest mistake we see clients make is a complete failure to file tax returns. Filing a return, even when money is owed, will start the statute of limitations clock, and may start the taxpayer on the path to dischargeability if he ever needs to file bankruptcy. Plus, as with other sections of this book, keep and retain documents to refer to years later if necessary.

About the Author

Shawn M. Yesner is a Florida native, born in Tampa and raised in Miami. After graduating from Florida State University with a Bachelor of Science degree in Accounting, Shawn enrolled in the Cumberland School of Law, Samford University, graduating with a Juris Doctor (J.D.) Degree in 1998.

Prior to starting his own practice, Shawn was an associate attorney at one of the largest lender foreclosure firms in Florida. There Shawn learned how to prosecute foreclosures quickly and efficiently, representing such lenders as Freddie Mac, Department of Veteran's Affairs (VA), Chase, Countrywide, and many other subprime lenders in all aspects for foreclosure litigation, bankruptcy, loss mitigation negotiations, and title insurance/title litigation.

In 2004, Shawn left the plaintiff's side of the practice to form a law firm focused on helping homeowners keep their homes. After building a successful multi-practice firm, Shawn founded Yesner Law, P.L., again with the focus of helping homeowners save their home or get rid of their home while incurring minimal liability.

Shawn has been a speaker at multiple Continuing Legal Education Seminars, Realtor® Education Seminars and Networking Seminars sponsored by Law Review CLE, National Business Institute (NBI), the American Bankruptcy Institute (ABI), Business Network International (BNI), Tampa Bay Business Owners (TBBO), The Florida Podcasters Association (FPA), Podfest Multimedia Expo, and has authored an article entitled "Loan Modifications Can Help Borrowers Keep Their Homes" as part of a book titled *Florida Foreclosure: What Lawyers Need to Know Now* published by Thomson Reuters in 2009. Among his affiliations, Shawn is a member of:

- The Florida Bar Real Property Probate & Trust Law Section
- Tampa Bay Bankruptcy Bar Association (TBBBA)

- National Association of Consumer Bankruptcy Attorneys (NACBA)
- American Bankruptcy Institute (ABI)
- Leadership Tampa Bay, Class of 2013
- Business Network International (BNI)
- Florida Podcasters Association (FPA)
- Safety Harbor Athletic Club (SHAC)

Shawn serves his Tampa Bay community as a volunteer pro bono attorney for the Stetson University College of Law Veterans Law Institute, and the St. Petersburg Bar Association Community Law Program. Shawn has also contributed pro bono hours for the Middle District of Florida Bankruptcy Court Pro Bono Clinic. He is also active within his home community, serving on the Variance Committee for the Westchase Community Association, and as an assistant soccer coach for the Westchase Soccer Association, and YMCA youth basketball. Shawn runs between three and four miles twice a week, and regularly participates or sponsors 5k races. Shawn, his wife and two sons live in Westchase, FL.

The Crushing Debt Podcast

My podcast came about because of peer pressure. Just kidding. My SEO guys kept telling me, "Shawn, we need more content!" I could not find the time to sit and write a blog (ironic that I found the time to write a book …). I would catch myself talking in the car describing all the stuff I would write about in my blog. I would speak it repeatedly to commit it to memory. What was I going to write about? Where was I going to insert the humor? Where would one article end, and another begin? Over and over until I had memorized the information I wanted to capture on the page.

About that same time, I was a member of the Tampa Bay Business Owners, and the founder, Chris Krimitsos, and his wife, Katie, had just launched Katie's podcast Biz Women Rock. Chris was talking all about the virtues and values of podcasting; check out Chris's movie, *The Messengers, A Podcast Documentary*, on iTunes, Amazon, and other on-demand services to see the power of this medium.

The advice I received, and the advice I give to new podcasters - buy a microphone, fire that bad boy up, and start talking. The rest (editing, hosting, distributing) will take care of itself. Just make sure that you're starting a podcast for the right reasons and that the topic is one you're passionate about. If you're starting a podcast because you think you will monetize it, you're starting it for all the wrong reasons. Just recently, my podcast has produced clients, but that return on investment took more than a hundred and fifteen episodes spread over nearly three years!

So, in November 2015, The Crushing Debt Podcast was launched! We're now on Apple Podcasts, Spotify, Stitcher, Google Play, iHeart Radio, and other podcast players. In addition, the podcast can be found on Echo products (Alexa), Google Voice products ("hey, Google") and your iPhone (Siri) - the artificial intelligence products love the show! The podcast supports the lawfirm by helping to eliminate the financial bullies in your life, with the message that "Everything will be okay."

The irony is that my blog has become more consistent (not as consistent as the podcast release - every Thursday morning at 6 AM Eastern Time), I have a TON of content available for my clients, and all of my social media now cross promotes: my Facebook Live's promote upcoming guests, transcription of shows become blogs, blogs were then used to write this book, the podcast will support book sales, social media will promote the book and the podcast, etc.

You would do me a huge favor by subscribing to the show and leaving us a rating or review (and you would do me a huge favor by reviewing this book too!).

Acknowledgements

Sitting here, late at night, hacking away at my iPad to get a draft that I can transfer to Word and then edit, I'm struck by the love and support I get daily from:

My family. My wife and kids are the reason I am here. I've known since high school I wanted to be an attorney. I've known for longer than that, that I wanted to be a husband and father. My wife keeps me grounded and my boys keep me young. My sister, brother-in-law and niece always make sure to knock me down a peg, in a loving and non-bullying way, and always out of love.

My mom for always loving me, no matter what – they say that sons will always be momma's boys, I see it with my boys and my wife, and it is true about me and my mom.

My dad for being my hero.

My co-workers. Yeah I'm the boss, but without the people in my office, who help me consistently, I would have no time to do anything. They started as my staff, they became my equals, and now they're part of the family.

FPA. The Florida Podcasters Association in Tampa was the genesis of the podcast, which created the book. In no particular order, with their podcasts in parenthesis, Chris Krimitsos (*Conference Cash Flow Podcast* and *Story Jam Theater*), Katie Krimitsos (*Biz Women Rock*), Gabriel Aluisy (*Private Club Radio, Golf Radio Network*), Tyler & Jill Sheff (*The Cash Flow Guys*), Polly Bauer (*Swipe! The Podcast*), Bruce Wawrzyniak (*Now Hear This Entertainment, Tascam Talkback*), Niel Guilarte (*All Things Post*), Rob Kellog (*Brewin' Up Business*), the Podfather Steve Cherubino (*The EDM Producer Podcast*), Jason Hewitt (*History of the Brand*), Lee Silverstein (*We Have Cancer*), and the rest of the FPA who have inspired me, or kicked me in the rear end, as needed.

BNI. Without BNI, I would have no idea how to network or grow a business (plus the podcast, and a speaking career). As with FPA, too many to mention, but a few stand out: Clay Caire, Tom Fleming, Tiffanie & Rob Kellog, Rich Ficca, Jason Avery, Robin Lavitch, Lee Carr, and many, many others who have passed me a referral, helped a client, friend or acquaintance of mine, and lived in the space of BNI's two-word philosophy of Givers Gain®.

They say it takes a village. When it came to editing I didn't have a village, I had a city to help me. I was overwhelmed when I asked for help in editing this book and got dozens of offers of help. Some reviewed just a chapter or two, others reviewed the entire book. Thank you all!

All the rest of my friends, who have always supported me. Thank you all for helping me to realize that I am not alone and being bullied. I have the backing of literally thousands of people. You all now inspire me to help eliminate the financial bullies threatening my clients, so they know, like I do, that there are always options, and everything is going to be okay.

Goodnight …

Index